Prayer Journal

For Women

52 WEEK
GUIDED SCRIPTURE DEVOTION
NOTEBOOK

· ·

For Beautiful Women Of God!

God HEARS you, God SEES you, God LOVES you!

2021 PUBLISHED BY RANT PRESS HOUSE
978-0-578-97876-5

This Journal Belongs
To:

. . . .

• • • • • • • • • • • • • • • •

WEEK 1

Date:

Today's Verse

Lord teach me

I am thankful for

Prayer Requests

Date:

Prayer Journal

FOR WOMEN

And if we know that he hears us—whatever we ask—we know that we have what we asked of him. 1 John 5:15

_____

_____

_____

_____

_____

_____

_____

_____

_____

_____

_____

_____

_____

_____

_____

_____

_____

_____

_____

_____

_____

_____

_____

WEEK 2

Date:

Today's Verse

Lord teach me

I am thankful for

Prayer Requests

Date:

Prayer Journal
FOR WOMEN

Rejoice always, pray continually, give thanks in all circumstances; for this is God's will for you in Christ Jesus.
1 Thessalonians 5:16-18

WEEK 3

Date:

Today's Verse

Lord teach me

I am thankful for

Prayer Requests

Date:

Prayer Journal

FOR WOMEN

Do not be anxious about anything, but in every situation, by prayer and petition, with thanksgiving, present your requests to God. And the peace of God, which transcends all understanding, will guard your hearts and your minds in Christ Jesus.
Philippians 4:6-7

WEEK 4

Today's Verse

Lord teach me

I am thankful for

Prayer Requests

Date:

Prayer Journal

FOR WOMEN

This is the confidence we have in approaching God: that if we ask anything according to
his will, he hears us.

1 John 5:14

WEEK 5

Date:

Today's Verse

Lord teach me

I am thankful for

Prayer Requests

Date:

Prayer Journal

FOR WOMEN

Devote yourselves to prayer, being watchful and thankful.
Colossians 4:2

_____

_____

_____

_____

_____

_____

_____

_____

_____

_____

_____

_____

_____

_____

_____

_____

_____

_____

_____

_____

_____

_____

_____

_____

WEEK 6

Today's Verse

Lord teach me

I am thankful for

Prayer Requests

Date:

Prayer Journal
FOR WOMEN

Therefore I tell you, whatever you ask for in prayer, believe that you have received it, and it will be yours.

Mark 11:24

_____

_____

_____

_____

_____

_____

_____

_____

_____

_____

_____

_____

_____

_____

_____

_____

_____

_____

_____

_____

_____

_____

_____

WEEK 7

Date:

Today's Verse

Lord teach me

I am thankful for

Prayer Requests

Date:

Prayer Journal

FOR WOMEN

Then you will call on me and come and pray to me, and I will listen to you.
Jeremiah 29:12

_____

_____

_____

_____

_____

_____

_____

_____

_____

_____

_____

_____

_____

_____

_____

_____

_____

_____

_____

_____

_____

_____

_____

WEEK 8

Date:

Today's Verse

Lord teach me

I am thankful for

Prayer Requests

Date:

Prayer Journal

FOR WOMEN

Be joyful in hope, patient in affliction, faithful in prayer.
Romans 12:12

WEEK 9

Date:

Today's Verse

Lord teach me

I am thankful for

Prayer Requests

Date:

FOR WOMEN

The Lord is near to all who call on him,
to all who call on him in truth.
Psalm 145:18

_____

_____

_____

_____

_____

_____

_____

_____

_____

_____

_____

_____

_____

_____

_____

_____

_____

_____

_____

_____

_____

_____

_____

_____

WEEK 10

Date:

Today's Verse

Lord teach me

I am thankful for

Prayer Requests

Date:

Prayer Journal

FOR WOMEN

And when you pray, do not keep on babbling like pagans, for they think they will be
heard because of their many words.

Matthew 6:7

WEEK 11

Date:

Today's Verse

Lord teach me

I am thankful for

Prayer Requests

Prayer Journal

FOR WOMEN

'Call to me and I will answer you and tell you great and unsearchable things you do not know.'

Jeremiah 33:3

_____

_____

_____

_____

_____

_____

_____

_____

_____

_____

_____

_____

_____

_____

_____

_____

_____

_____

_____

_____

_____

_____

WEEK 12

Today's Verse

Lord teach me

I am thankful for

Prayer Requests

Date:

Prayer Journal

FOR WOMEN

"For where two or three gather in my name, there am I with them."
Matthew 18:20

WEEK 13

Date:

Today's Verse

Lord teach me

I am thankful for

Prayer Requests

Date:

Prayer Journal

FOR WOMEN

Let us then approach God's throne of grace with confidence, so that we may receive
mercy and find grace to help us in our time of need.
Hebrews 4:16

WEEK 14

Date:

Today's Verse

Lord teach me

I am thankful for

Prayer Requests

Date:

Prayer Journal

FOR WOMEN

But when you pray, go into your room, close the door and pray to your Father, who is
unseen. Then your Father, who sees what is done in secret, will reward you.
Matthew 6:6

_____

_____

_____

_____

_____

_____

_____

_____

_____

_____

_____

_____

_____

_____

_____

_____

_____

_____

_____

_____

_____

_____

_____

_____

_____

WEEK 15

Date:

Today's Verse

Lord teach me

I am thankful for

Prayer Requests

Date:

Prayer Journal
FOR WOMEN

About midnight Paul and Silas were praying and singing hymns to God, and the other prisoners were listening to them.
Acts 16:25

_____

_____

_____

_____

_____

_____

_____

_____

_____

_____

_____

_____

_____

_____

_____

_____

_____

_____

_____

_____

_____

_____

_____

_____

WEEK 16

Date:

Today's Verse

Lord teach me

I am thankful for

Prayer Requests

Date:

Prayer Journal

FOR WOMEN

In my distress I called to the Lord;
I cried to my God for help. From his temple he heard my voice;
my cry came before him, into his ears.
Psalm 18:6

WEEK 17

Date:

Today's Verse

Lord teach me

I am thankful for

Prayer Requests

Date:

Prayer Journal
FOR WOMEN

Therefore confess your sins to each other and pray for each other so that you may be healed. The prayer of a righteous person is powerful and effective.
James 5:16

WEEK 18

Today's Verse

Lord teach me

I am thankful for

Prayer Requests

Date:

Prayer Journal
FOR WOMEN

But when you ask, you must believe and not doubt, because the one who doubts is like a
wave of the sea, blown and tossed by the wind.

James 1:6

_____

_____

_____

_____

_____

_____

_____

_____

_____

_____

_____

_____

_____

_____

_____

_____

_____

_____

_____

_____

_____

_____

_____

WEEK 19

Today's Verse

Date:

Lord teach me

I am thankful for

Prayer Requests

Date:

Prayer Journal

FOR WOMEN

You did not choose me, but I chose you and appointed you so that you might go and bear fruit—fruit that will last—and so that whatever you ask in my name the Father will give you.

John 15:16

_____

_____

_____

_____

_____

_____

_____

_____

_____

_____

_____

_____

_____

_____

_____

_____

_____

_____

_____

_____

_____

_____

WEEK 20

Today's Verse

Lord teach me

I am thankful for

Prayer Requests

Date:

Prayer Journal

FOR WOMEN

But when you ask, you must believe and not doubt, because the one who doubts is like a
wave of the sea, blown and tossed by the wind.

James 1:6

_____

_____

_____

_____

_____

_____

_____

_____

_____

_____

_____

_____

_____

_____

_____

_____

_____

_____

_____

_____

_____

_____

_____

WEEK 21

Date:

Today's Verse

Lord teach me

I am thankful for

Prayer Requests

Date:

Prayer Journal

FOR WOMEN

The end of all things is near. Therefore be alert and of sober mind so that you may pray.
1 Peter 4:7

_____

_____

_____

_____

_____

_____

_____

_____

_____

_____

_____

_____

_____

_____

_____

_____

_____

_____

_____

_____

_____

_____

_____

_____

WEEK 22

Today's Verse

Lord teach me

I am thankful for

Prayer Requests

Date:

Prayer Journal
FOR WOMEN

My prayer is not that you take them out of the world but that you protect them from the evil one. John 17:15

_____
_____
_____
_____
_____
_____
_____
_____
_____
_____
_____
_____
_____
_____
_____
_____
_____
_____
_____
_____
_____
_____

WEEK 23

Today's Verse

Date:

Lord teach me

I am thankful for

Prayer Requests

Prayer Journal

FOR WOMEN

One of those days Jesus went out to a mountainside to pray, and spent the night praying to God. Luke 6:12

_____

_____

_____

_____

_____

_____

_____

_____

_____

_____

_____

_____

_____

_____

_____

_____

_____

_____

_____

_____

_____

_____

WEEK 24

Date:

Today's Verse

Lord teach me

I am thankful for

Prayer Requests

Date:

Prayer Journal
FOR WOMEN

Devote yourselves to prayer, being watchful and thankful. Colossians 4:2

WEEK 25

Date:

Today's Verse

Lord teach me

I am thankful for

Prayer Requests

Date:

Prayer Journal

FOR WOMEN

I can do all things through him who strengthens me.
Philippians 4:13

_____

_____

_____

_____

_____

_____

_____

_____

_____

_____

_____

_____

_____

_____

_____

_____

_____

_____

_____

_____

_____

_____

_____

WEEK 26

Today's Verse

Lord teach me

I am thankful for

Prayer Requests

Date:

Prayer Journal

FOR WOMEN

Fear not, for I am with you; be not dismayed, for I am your God; I will strengthen you, I
will help you, I will uphold you with my righteous right hand.
Isaiah 41:10

WEEK 27

Date:

Today's Verse

Lord teach me

I am thankful for

Prayer Requests

Date:

Prayer Journal

FOR WOMEN

Isaiah 40:31 But they who wait for the Lord shall renew their strength; they shall mount up with wings like eagles; they shall run and not be weary; they shall walk and not faint.

WEEK 28

Today's Verse

Lord teach me

I am thankful for

Prayer Requests

Date:

Prayer Journal

FOR WOMEN

1 Corinthians 10:13 No temptation has overtaken you that is not common to man. God is faithful, and he will not let you be tempted beyond your ability, but with the temptation he will also provide the way of escape, that you may be able to endure it.

_____

_____

_____

_____

_____

_____

_____

_____

_____

_____

_____

_____

_____

_____

_____

_____

_____

_____

_____

_____

_____

_____

_____

WEEK 29

Today's Verse

Lord teach me

I am thankful for

Prayer Requests

Date:

Prayer Journal

FOR WOMEN

Exodus 15:2 The Lord is my strength and my song, and he has become my salvation; this is my God, and I will praise him, my father's God, and I will exalt him.

_____

_____

_____

_____

_____

_____

_____

_____

_____

_____

_____

_____

_____

_____

_____

_____

_____

_____

_____

_____

_____

_____

WEEK 30

Date:

Today's Verse

Lord teach me

I am thankful for

Prayer Requests

Date:

Prayer Journal

FOR WOMEN

Ephesians 6:10 Finally, be strong in the Lord and in the strength of his might.

WEEK 31

Date:

Today's Verse

Lord teach me

I am thankful for

Prayer Requests

Date:

Prayer Journal

FOR WOMEN

Deuteronomy 20:4 For the Lord your God is he who goes with you to fight for you against your enemies, to give you the victory.

WEEK 32

Today's Verse

Lord teach me

I am thankful for

Prayer Requests

Date:

Prayer Journal

FOR WOMEN

Joshua 1:9 Have I not commanded you? Be strong and courageous. Do not be frightened, and do not be dismayed, for the Lord your God is with you wherever you go.

WEEK 33

Date:

Today's Verse

Lord teach me

I am thankful for

Prayer Requests

Date:

Prayer Journal

FOR WOMEN

2 Timothy 1:7 For God gave us a spirit not of fear but of power and love and self-control.

WEEK 34

Today's Verse

Lord teach me

I am thankful for

Prayer Requests

Date:

Prayer Journal

FOR WOMEN

Isaiah 12:2 "Behold, God is my salvation; I will trust, and will not be afraid; for the Lord
God is my strength and my song, and he has become my salvation."

_____

_____

_____

_____

_____

_____

_____

_____

_____

_____

_____

_____

_____

_____

_____

_____

_____

_____

_____

_____

_____

_____

WEEK 35

Date:

Today's Verse

Lord teach me

I am thankful for

Prayer Requests

Date:

Prayer Journal

FOR WOMEN

Matthew 11:28 Come to me, all who labor and are heavy laden, and I will give you rest.

WEEK 36

Today's Verse

Lord teach me

I am thankful for

Prayer Requests

Date:

Prayer Journal

FOR WOMEN

Isaiah 40:29 He gives power to the faint, and to him who has no might he increases strength.

WEEK 37

Today's Verse

Lord teach me

I am thankful for

Prayer Requests

Date:

Prayer Journal

FOR WOMEN

Psalm 27:1 Of David. The Lord is my light and my salvation; whom shall I fear? The Lord is the stronghold of my life; of whom shall I be afraid?

_____

_____

_____

_____

_____

_____

_____

_____

_____

_____

_____

_____

_____

_____

_____

_____

_____

_____

_____

_____

_____

_____

_____

WEEK 38

Date:

Today's Verse

Lord teach me

I am thankful for

Prayer Requests

Date:

Prayer Journal
FOR WOMEN

Psalm 31:24 Be strong, and let your heart take courage, all you who wait for the Lord!

_____

_____

_____

_____

_____

_____

_____

_____

_____

_____

_____

_____

_____

_____

_____

_____

_____

_____

_____

_____

_____

_____

WEEK 39

Date:

Today's Verse

Lord teach me

I am thankful for

Prayer Requests

Date:

Prayer Journal

FOR WOMEN

Psalm 73:26 My flesh and my heart may fail, but God is the strength of my heart and my portion forever.

WEEK 40

Date:

Today's Verse

Lord teach me

I am thankful for

Prayer Requests

Prayer Journal

FOR WOMEN

2 Corinthians 12:9 But he said to me, "My grace is sufficient for you, for my power is made perfect in weakness." Therefore I will boast all the more gladly of my weaknesses, so that the power of Christ may rest upon me.

WEEK 41

Today's Verse

Lord teach me

I am thankful for

Prayer Requests

Date:

Prayer Journal

FOR WOMEN

Mark 12:30 And you shall love the Lord your God with all your heart and with all your
soul and with all your mind and with all your strength.'

WEEK 42

Today's Verse

Date:

Lord teach me

I am thankful for

Prayer Requests

Date:

Prayer Journal

FOR WOMEN

Nehemiah 8:10 Then he said to them, "Go your way. Eat the fat and drink sweet wine and send portions to anyone who has nothing ready, for this day is holy to our Lord. And do not be grieved, for the joy of the Lord is your strength."

WEEK 43

Today's Verse

Lord teach me

I am thankful for

Prayer Requests

Date:

Prayer Journal

FOR WOMEN

Psalm 46:1 To the choirmaster. Of the Sons of Korah. According to Alamoth. A Song. God is our refuge and strength, a very present help in trouble.

_____

_____

_____

_____

_____

_____

_____

_____

_____

_____

_____

_____

_____

_____

_____

_____

_____

_____

_____

_____

_____

WEEK 44

Date:

Today's Verse

Lord teach me

I am thankful for

Prayer Requests

Date:

Prayer Journal
FOR WOMEN

Habakkuk 3:19 God, the Lord, is my strength; he makes my feet like the deer's; he makes me tread on my high places. To the choirmaster: with stringed instruments.

WEEK 45

Today's Verse

Date:

Lord teach me

I am thankful for

Prayer Requests

Date:

Prayer Journal
FOR WOMEN

Psalm 29:11 May the Lord give strength to his people! May the Lord bless his people with peace.

WEEK 46

Date:

Today's Verse

Lord teach me

I am thankful for

Prayer Requests

Date:

Prayer Journal

FOR WOMEN

John 16:33 I have said these things to you, that in me you may have peace. In the world you will have tribulation. But take heart; I have overcome the world."

WEEK 47

Date:

Today's Verse

Lord teach me

I am thankful for

Prayer Requests

WEEK 48

Date:

Today's Verse

Lord teach me

I am thankful for

Prayer Requests

WEEK 49

Today's Verse

Lord teach me

I am thankful for

Prayer Requests

WEEK 50

Today's Verse

Date:

Lord teach me

I am thankful for

Prayer Requests

WEEK 51

Date:

Today's Verse

Lord teach me

I am thankful for

Prayer Requests

WEEK 52

Date:

Today's Verse

Reflecction

_____
_____
_____
_____
_____
_____
_____
_____
_____
_____
_____
_____
_____
_____
_____
_____
_____
_____
_____
_____
_____

Made in the USA
Columbia, SC
24 June 2022

62217170R00057